Music and Lyrics by
STEPHEN SONDHEIM

Book by
JAMES GOLDMAN

VOCAL SCORE

Piano reduction by
Robert Noeltner

D1211467

"FOLLIES"

Produced by
HAROLD PRINCE

In association with RUTH MITCHELL
First Performance April 4, 1971 at the Winter Garden
Production directed by HAROLD PRINCE AND MICHAEL BENNETT
Choreography by MICHAEL BENNETT
Scenic Production Designed by BORIS ARONSON
Costumes Designed by FLORENCE KLOTZ
Lighting by THARON MUSSER
Musical Direction by HAROLD HASTINGS
Orchestrations by JONATHAN TUNICK
Dance Music Arranged by JOHN BERKMAN

CAST OF CHARACTERS
(In order of appearance)

MAJOR-DOMO . . . . Dick Latessa
SALLY DURANT PLUMMER . . . . Dorothy Collins
YOUNG SALLY . . . . Marti Rolph
CHRISTINE CRANE . . . . Ethel Barrymore Colt
WILLY WHEELER . . . . Fred Kelly
STELLA DEEMS . . . . Mary McCarty
MAX DEEMS . . . . John J. Martin
HEIDI SCHILLER . . . . Justine Johnston
CHAUFFEUR . . . . John Grigas
MEREDITH LANE . . . . Sheila Smith
CHET RICHARDS . . . . Peter Walker
ROSCOE . . . . Michael Bartlett
DEEDEE WEST . . . . Helon Blount
SANDRA DONOVAN . . . . Sonja Levkova
HATTIE WALKER . . . . Ethel Shutta
YOUNG HATTIE . . . . Mary Jane Houdina
EMILY WHITMAN . . . . Marcie Stringer
THEODORE WHITMAN . . . . Charles Welch
VINCENT . . . . Victor Griffin
VANESSA . . . . Jayne Turner
YOUNG VINCENT . . . . Michael Misita
YOUNG VANESSA . . . . Graciela Daniele
SOLANGE LaFITTE . . . . Fifi D'Orsay
CARLOTTA CAMPION . . . . Yvonne De Carlo
PHYLLIS ROGERS STONE . . . . Alexis Smith
BENJAMIN STONE . . . . John McMartin
YOUNG PHYLLIS . . . . Virginia Sandifur
YOUNG BEN . . . . Kurt Peterson
BUDDY PLUMMER . . . . Gene Nelson
YOUNG BUDDY . . . . Harvey Evans
DIMITRI WEISMANN . . . . Arnold Moss
KEVIN . . . . Ralph Nelson
YOUNG HEIDI . . . . Victoria Mallory
PARTY MUSICIANS . . . . Taft Jordan, Aaron Bell,
Charles Spies, Robert Curtis
SHOWGIRLS . . . . .Suzanne Briggs, Trudy Carson, Kathie Dalton,
Ursula Maschmeyer, Linda Perkins, Margot Travers
SINGERS AND DANCERS . . . . Graciela Daniele, Mary Jane Houdina,
Rita O'Connor, Julie Pars, Suzanne Rogers, Roy Barry,
Steve Boockvor, Michael Misita, Joseph Nelson,
Ralph Nelson, Ken Urmston, Donald Weissmuller

SCENE: A party on the stage of the Weismann Theatre
TIME: Tonight

There will be no Intermission

MUSICAL NUMBERS

1—THE FOLLY OF LOVE

   "Loveland" . . . . Sung by The Ensemble
   The Spirit Of First Love . . . . Miss Kathie Dalton
   The Spirit Of Young Love . . . . Miss Margot Travers
   The Spirit Of True Love . . . . Miss Suzanne Briggs
   The Spirit Of Pure Love . . . . Miss Trudy Carson
   The Spirit Of Romantic Love . . . . Miss Linda Perkins
   The Spirit Of Eternal Love . . . . Miss Ursula Maschmeyer

2—THE FOLLY OF YOUTH
   Scene—A Bower in Loveland
       "You're Gonna Love Tomorrow" . . . Sung by Mr. Ben Stone and Miss Phyllis Rogers
       "Love Will See Us Through" . . . Sung by Mr. Buddy Plummer and Miss Sally Durant

3—BUDDY'S FOLLY
   Scene—A Thoroughfare in Loveland
       "The God-Why-Don't-You-Love-Me Blues" . Sung and Danced by Mr. Buddy Plummer
       (With the Assistance of Miss Suzanne Rogers and Miss Rita O'Connor)

4—SALLY'S FOLLY
   Scene—A Boudoir in Loveland
       "Losing My Mind" . . . . Sung by Mrs. Sally Durant Plummer

5—PHYLLIS'S FOLLY
   Scene—A Honky-Tonk in Loveland
       "The Story of Lucy and Jessie" . . . . Sung by Mrs. Phyllis Rogers Stone
       (Danced by Mrs. Stone and The Dancing Ensemble)

6—BEN'S FOLLY
   Scene—A Supper Club in Loveland
       "Live, Laugh, Love" . . . . Sung by Mr. Benjamin Stone
       (Danced by Mr. Stone and The Dancing Ensemble)

For Jim Goldman

FOLLIES
Prologue

No. 1

Music and Lyrics by
STEPHEN SONDHEIM

7

SALLY: It's going to be a lovely party. I'm so glad I came.

No. 1a

Overture

[Double time feel]

18

(PHILLIS and BEN enter)

Tpts.,Cls.,Str. - - *[Fade to Violin Solo as applause dies]*

YOUNG BUDDY:

Hey, up there, 'Way up there, Whad-da-ya say up there?

(BUDDY enters)

Beautiful Girls

Cue: **WEISMANN:** I don't trust any music under thirty -- Maestro, if you please!

Maestoso
[Stage Band till Bar 37]

Hats off, here they come, those Beau-ti-ful girls.

That's what you've been wait-ing for.

Na - ture nev-er fash-ioned a flow-er so fair.

No rose can com - pare, Noth - ing re - spec - ta - ble

half so de - lec - ta - ble. Cheer them in their glo - ry, Dia - monds and

(Hp. cued)

(Stage Tpt.)

pearls, Dazz - ling jew - els by the score.

(cued in W. W.)

(Stage Tpt.)

This is what beau - ty can be,

(Stage Tpt.)

71 ENTIRE COMPANY:

Care - ful, here's the home of Beau - ti - ful girls,

Where your rea - son is un - done.

Beau - ty can't be hin - dered from tak - ing its toll.

You may lose con - trol. Faced with these Lo - re - leis,

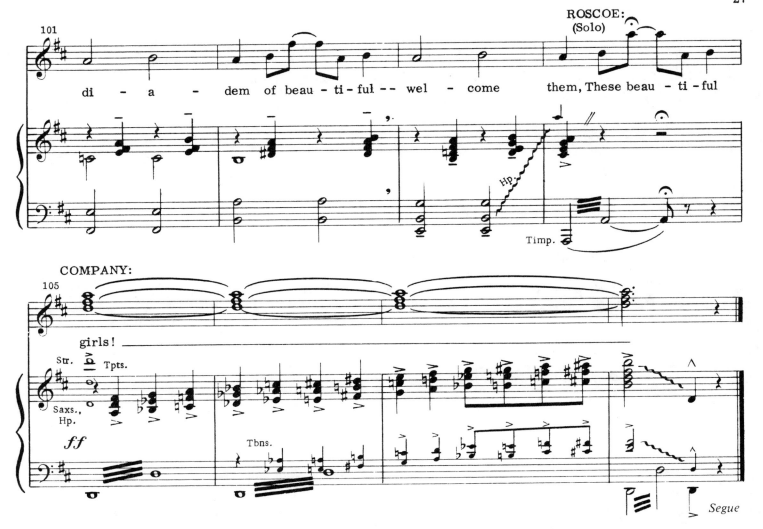

No. 2a

Beautiful Girls
(Underscore)

[Stage Band]

Start as stage breaks (tutti f) for 8 bars. Then at cue Tpt. joins in only for swells for no more than 2 measures. The cues come about a chorus apart, so slightly more than 4 choruses are played. Stop after 4th cue: SALLY: Ta-da!

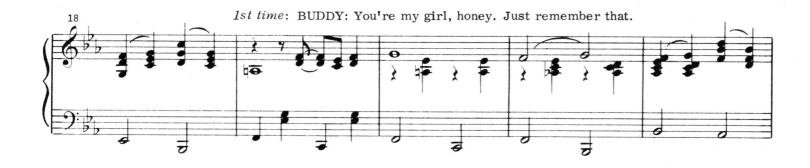

No. 3

Don't Look At Me-Verse

Cue: SALLY: Ta-da!

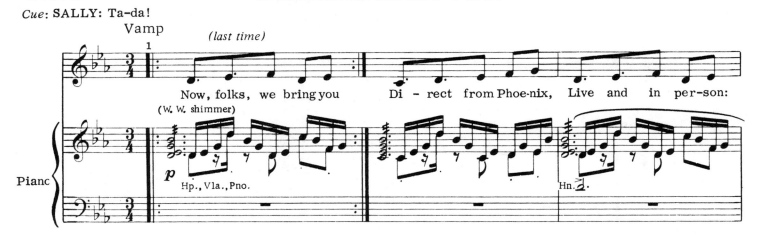

Now, folks, we bring you Di-rect from Phoe-nix, Live and in per-son:

Sal-ly Du-rant! Here she is at last,

[Vamp] Stop at cue: PHYLLIS: Sally, it is you, isn't it?

Twin-kle in her eye....

Segue

No. 3a

Who's That Woman?
(Underscore)

Cue: PHYLLIS: If you can't, I can.

[Stage Band]

Trumpet plays lead (p) first chorus. Piano plays lead in second chorus until cue for "swell" about bar [17].
Trumpet enters for one bar swell and drops out until segue to "Loveland".

Easy 4

At cue: **HATTIE**: My goodness, it was something. *Segue directly to "Loveland"*

No. 3b

Loveland
(Underscore)

[Stage Band]

Moderate 4
(Tpt. Solo)

Piano

pp

(Piano)

To Coda ✛

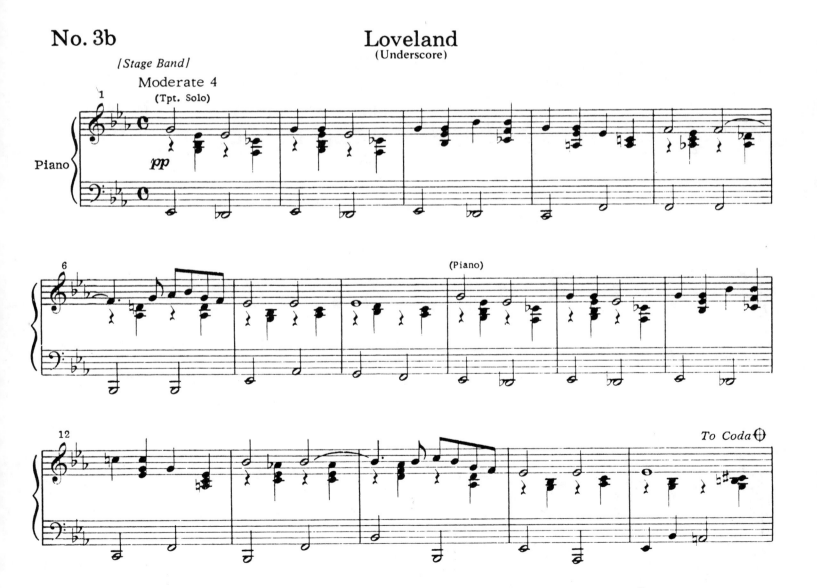

On cue: BUDDY: Hey, will you look at that -- *Segue white note gliss. to "One More Kiss"*

No. 3c

One More Kiss
(Underscore)

[Stage Band]

Moderate Waltz

Piano

Tpt. joins for 4 bar swell on cue: VINCENT: Styles change. You never know.

Add Tpt. and swell for 3-4 bars on cue: **HEIDI: What matters is the song.**

36

Add Tpt. and swell on cue: BEN: **I said the wrong things. Now I'm president of a foundation.**
(after 4 bar swell, Tpt. goes to pit orch.)
Stop at cue: SALLY: **Ben!**

No. 4

Cue: SALLY: Ben, it's me.

Don't Look At Me
(Sally, Ben)

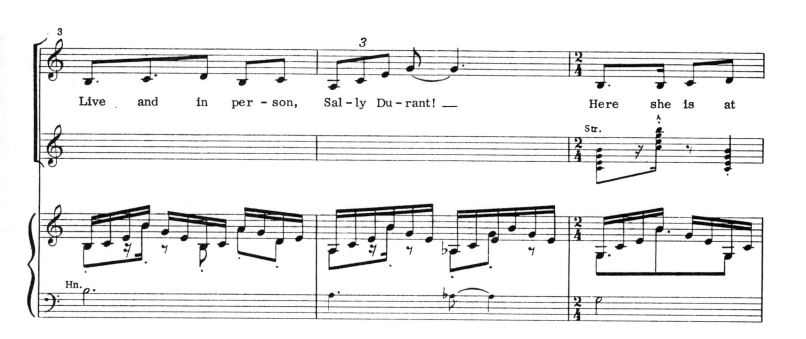

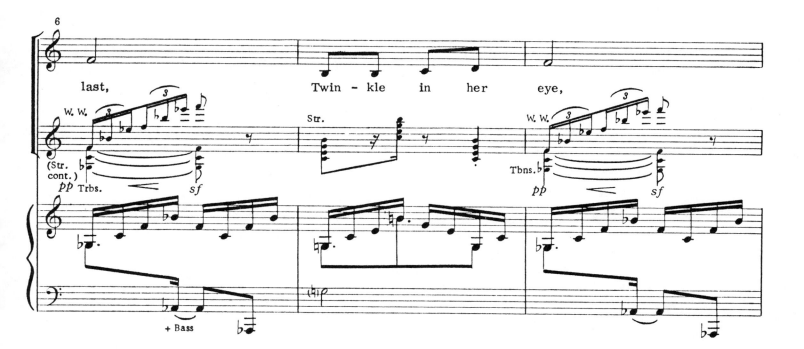

40

BEN: What we need
is a drink.

[Applause]

Segue to
Stage Band

No. 4a

Ah, Paris!
(Underscore)

Cue: After applause "Don't Look At Me"

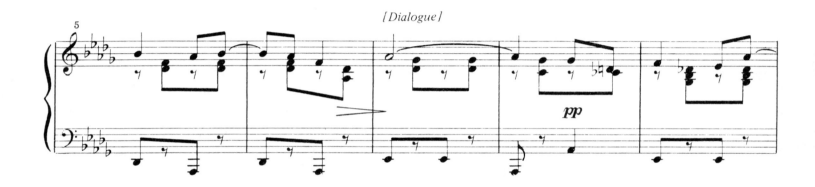

2nd time Swell on cue: BEN: I didn't think it showed.

1st time: Add Tpt. and swell on cue: CARLOTTA:
You want to hear the story of my life?   *Stay forte until winch bearing Buddy and Phyllis*

comes forward - then pp for more dialogue.

BUDDY: Stage door, call board -- what's so special?

No. 5   Waiting For The Girls Upstairs

(Buddy, Phyllis, Sally, Ben - young and old)

Cue: BUDDY: Waiting for the
girls to come down!

BUDDY: You always took (etc.)
... carved my name
here some place.

[Dialogue] cont. at cue:
BEN: ... face all
that again.

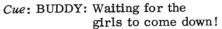

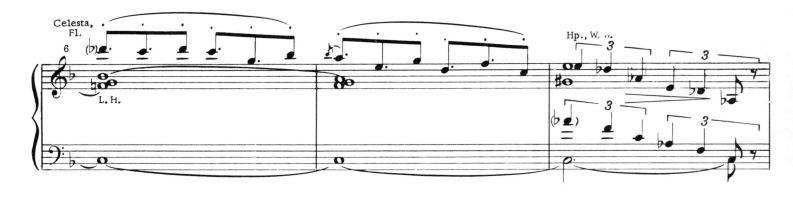

111

wait - ing for the boys _____ down - stairs.

Con Ped.

115

Agitato
+ W. W., Hp. 8va

SALLY:

Down ___ in a min - ute!

PHYLLIS:

Just ___

BUDDY:

You up there!

BEN:

You two up there!

mp

Str. trem. + Hn.

(+ Str.)

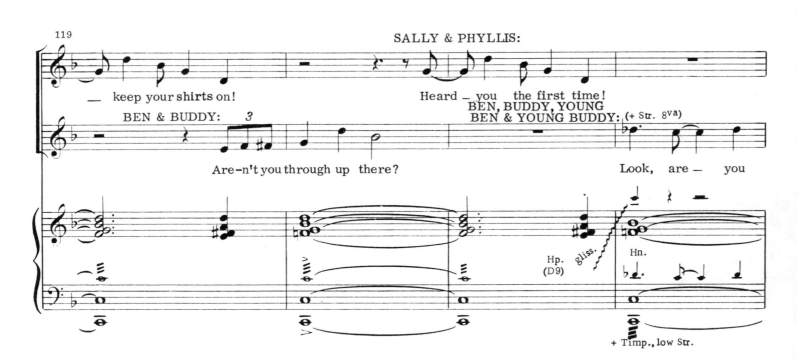

119

SALLY & PHYLLIS:

___ keep your shirts on!

Heard ___ you the first time!

BEN, BUDDY, YOUNG
BEN & YOUNG BUDDY: (+ Str. 8va)

BEN & BUDDY: 3

Are-n't you through up there?

Look, are — you

Hp.
(D9)

gliss.

Hn.

+ Timp., low Str.

60

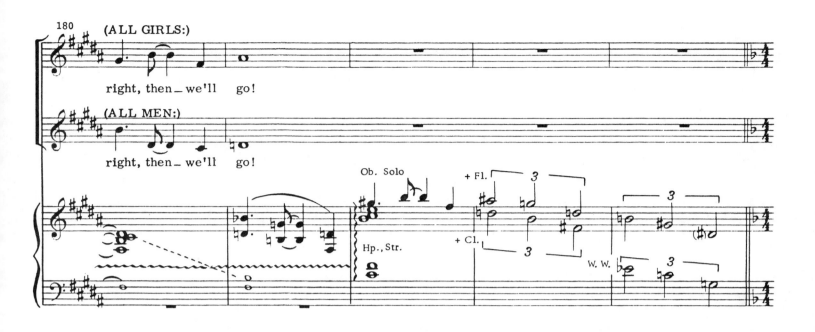

180 (ALL GIRLS:)
right, then — we'll go!

(ALL MEN:)
right, then — we'll go!

Ob. Solo
Hp., Str.
+ Fl.
+ Cl.
W. W.

185

Cls.
(Con Ped.)

189 BUDDY:
Wait-ing a-round — for the girls up-stairs, —

BEN:
Were-n't we chuck-le-heads then?

Tbn.
Cls.
(Cls. cont.)

SALLY & PHYLLIS:
Back there when one of the ma-jor e-vents Was wait-ing for the

BEN & BUDDY:
Back there when one of the ma-jor e-vents Was wait-ing for the girls,

(SALLY & PHYLLIS:)
girls, Wait-ing for the girls up -

(BEN & BUDDY:)
Wait-ing for the girls, Wait-ing for the girls up -

(SALLY & PHYLLIS:)
stairs.

(BEN & BUDDY:)
stairs.

(Con Ped.)

No. 5a

Fox-trot

Cue: Flash bulbs go off.
[Stage Band]

Moderately

Add Tpt. and Swell on cue: EMILY W.: I met you, didn't I?

Stop at cue: WEISSMANN: Do you want to be a star, my dear?

No. 6
Montage
(The Whitmans, Solange, and Hattie)

Cue: WEISMANN: Want to be a star, my dear?

Plunk-a-plink (kiss) Plank (kiss) Pit-y that it's not a hur-ri-

cane. _____ + Br.-- Lis-ten, plink, to the (kiss)(kiss) love-ly

rain.

SOLANGE:

New

Learn-ing how to sing and dance, __

Wait-ing for that one big chance __ to be in a show. _____

Gee, I'd like to be _____ on some mar-quee, _____ All twink - ling lights, _ a

spark to pierce the dark __ From Batt-'ry Park _____ to Wash - ing-ton Heights. _

Some day, may-be, _____ All my dreams will be re - paid. _

Hell, I'd e - ven play the maid ____ to be in a

show! _____ Say, Mis - ter Pro-duc - er, ___

I'm talk - ing to you, ___ sir. ____ I don't need a lot,

On - ly what I got, Plus a tube of grease-paint and a fol - low spot! _ I'm a

Broad - way Ba - by, _____ Slav - ing at a five and ten, _

Dream-ing of the great day when _ I'll be in a

show. _____

Broad-way Ba-by, _____ Mak-ing rounds all af-ter-noon, _____

Eat-ing at a greas-y spoon _____ to save on my dough. _____

[Solid 4]

At my ti-ny flat _____ there's just my cat, _____ a bed _____ and a chair. _

SOLANGE:

Still I'll stick it till _____ I'm on a bill _____ All o - ver Times Square, New

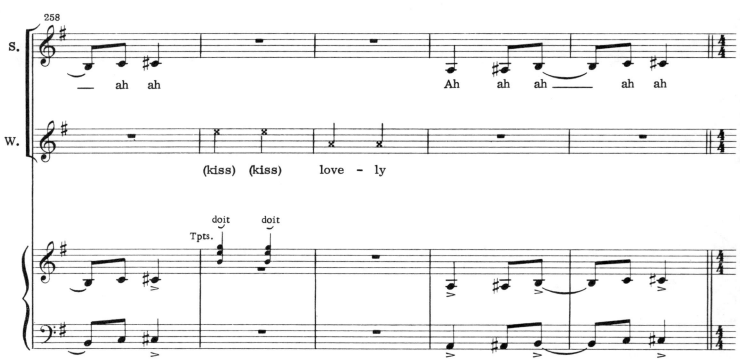

No. 7

The Road You Didn't Take
(Ben)

Cue: BEN: It's knowing what you want, that's the secret.

No. 8

Ah, Paris!-No. 2

Cue: SALLY: I even think I loved him once.

Cue: PHYLLIS: It might have mattered once.

[Rain On The Roof]

(ad lib. Bass fills)

Tpt. repeat until cue: PHYLLIS: ... I have $30,000 worth of Georgian silverware in my dining room.

Segue as one to [8a]

No. 8a

Beguine

PHYLLIS: -- and don't make waves.
(Cymbal as Pit Orch. enters)

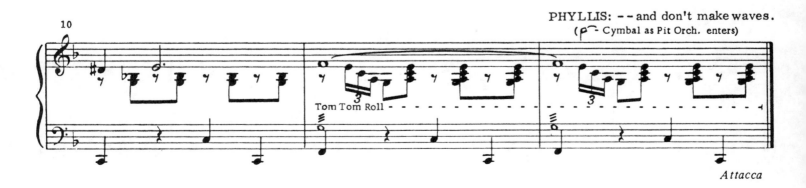

Tom Tom Roll - - - - - - - - - - -

Attacca

No. 9

Vincent And Vanessa

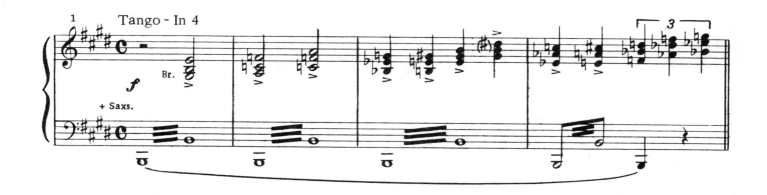

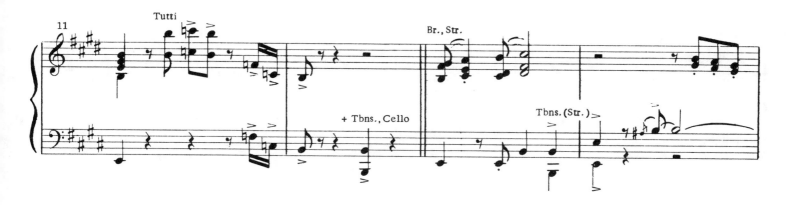

No. 10

In Buddy's Eyes
(Sally)

Cue: After applause from "Tango"

SALLY: ... and then the Follies closed... etc.

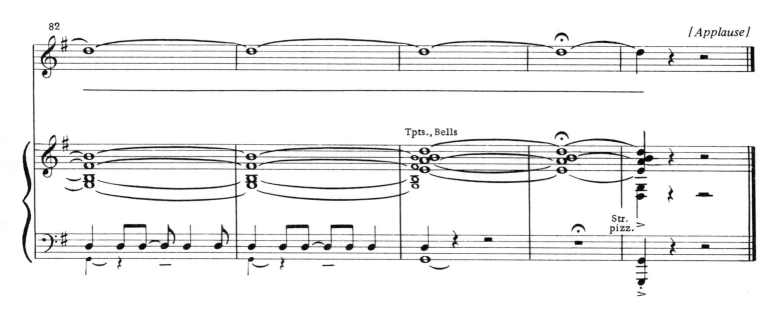

[Applause]

No. 11

Who's That Woman?

[Stage Band]

Cue: After applause from "Buddy's Eyes"

1st Chorus: Tpt. Lead   2nd Chorus: Piano - 1st 16 bars

Tpt. 2nd 16 bars

(Piano continues if more music is needed)

No. 12

(Pit Orch. cued to Bar 43)

Cue: STELLA: Hit it, baby!

Who's That Woman?
(Stella, Sally, Phyllis and Girls)

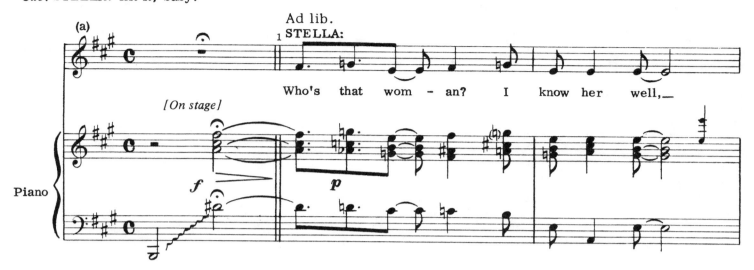

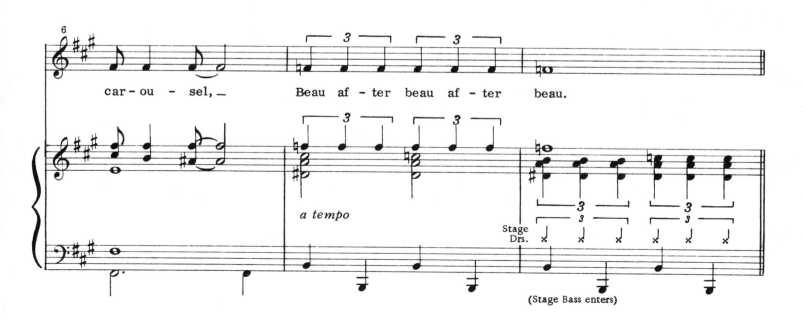

Segue
[*Stage Band*]

No. 12a

Fanfare

[Stage Band]

Cue: When lights go down after "Who's That Woman?"

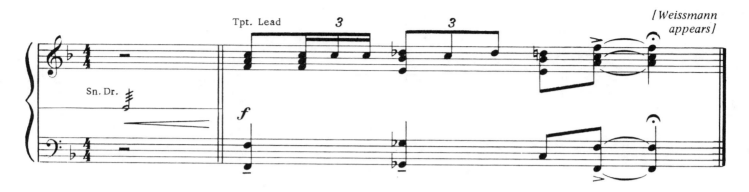

No. 13

Rain On The Roof

[Stage Band]

Cue: PHYLLIS: I don't suppose you play the drums?

No. 14

I'm Still Here

Cue: **CARLOTTA**: Whatcha gonna do?

Plush vel-vet some-times, Some-times just pret-zels and beer,___ But I'm here..

I've run the gam-ut, A to Z.___ Three cheers and dam-mit,

C'est la vie.___ I got thru' all of last year___ And I'm here._

Lord knows, at least I was there,___ And I'm

here. _____ Look who's here! _____ I'm still

here! _____

[Applause]

Segue
[Stage Band]

No. 14a   Underscore

[Stage Band]

Cue: After applause from "I'm Still Here"

Bass and Trumpet quietly improvise on the blues and stop when Young Sally begins to speak.

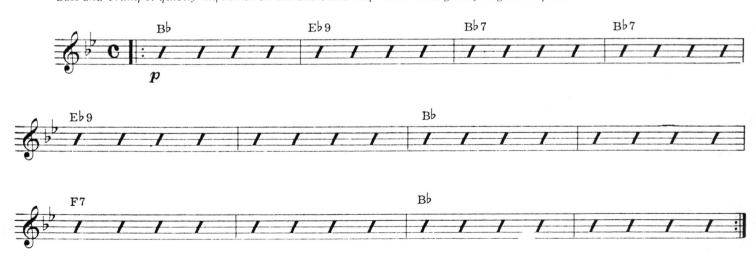

No. 15

Too Many Mornings

(Ben and Sally)

Cue: Young Sally slips into Ben's arms.

148

104
Sal - ly mov - ing to the bed, _____ Sal - ly rest - ing in {your my

107
arms _____ With your head a - gainst my head. _____
subito **p**
a tempo
+ Tpts.
Cls.
Ob. (Vln. cue)
p *a tempo*
Cello
Bs.

111
Vla. (Vln.)
(Cl. cue)
Muted Vln.
(Fl. cue)

115
+ Bells
(+ Vln. 2)
Hp.
Vla.
(Cl.)
Ped.
*

No. 16

The Right Girl
(Buddy)

Cue: **SALLY:** It's fine. We're going to be just fine.

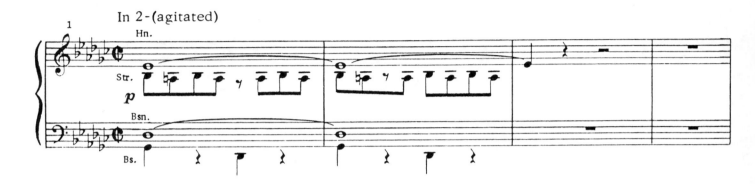

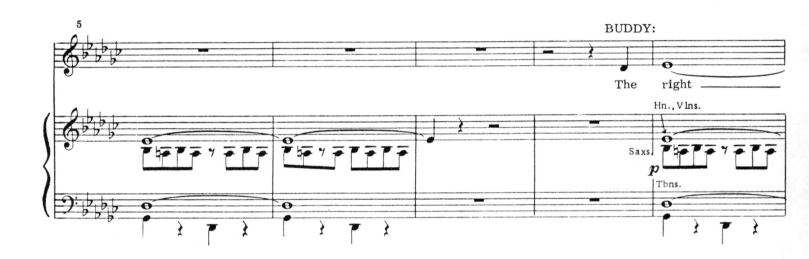

[Dance]

kay, babe,— what-ev er you say, babe,— You wan-na stay home!_____

You wan-na stay home!_____

No. 17

One More Kiss
(Young Heidi, Old Heidi)

Cue: CARLOTTA: Men are so sweet.

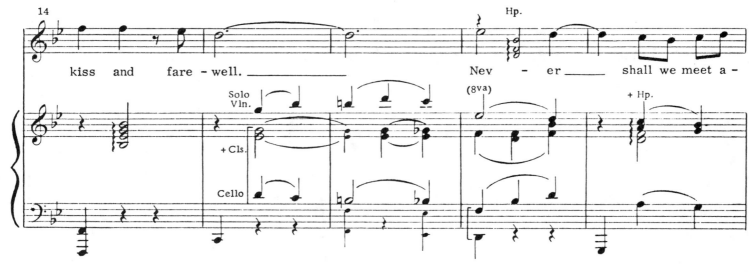

167

[Segue to bar [83]
on applause]

No. 18

Could I Leave You?
(Phyllis)

Cue: BEN: You, Stone! I know what you are.

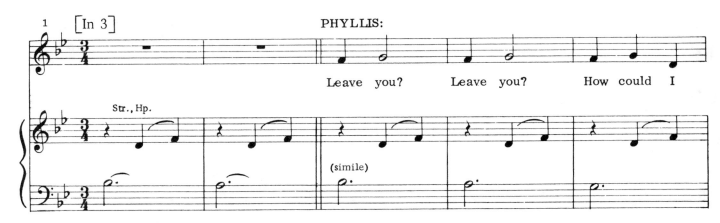

Leave you? Leave you? How could I

leave you? How could I go it a - lone? Could I wave the

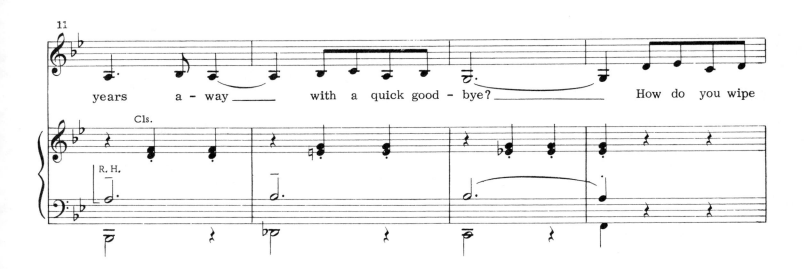

years a - way with a quick good - bye? How do you wipe

172

when I left long a - go, _____ love? _____

Could I leave you? No, the point is, Could

you leave me? Well, I guess you could

leave me the house, Leave me the flat,

No 19-1

Loveland
(Company)

Cue: YOUNG PHYLLIS: Can't we have one?
Can't we try?

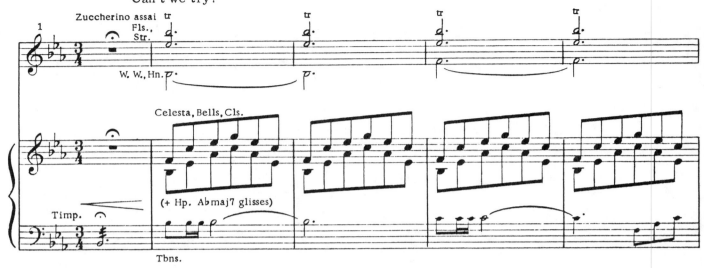

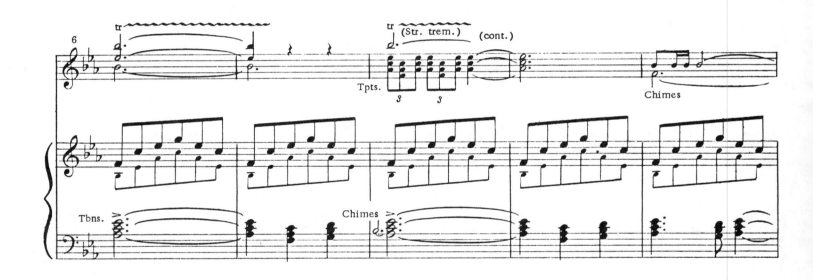

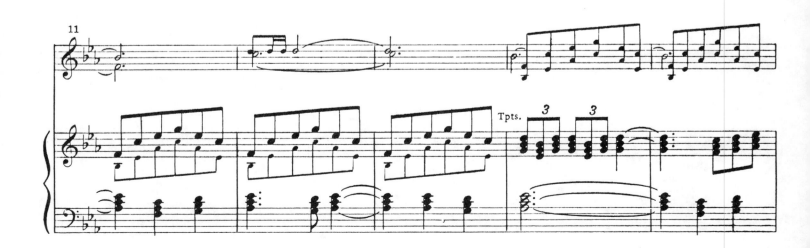

186

No. 19-2

You're Gonna Love Tomorrow
(Young Phyllis, Ben, Sally, Buddy)

Cue: *After applause from "Loveland"*

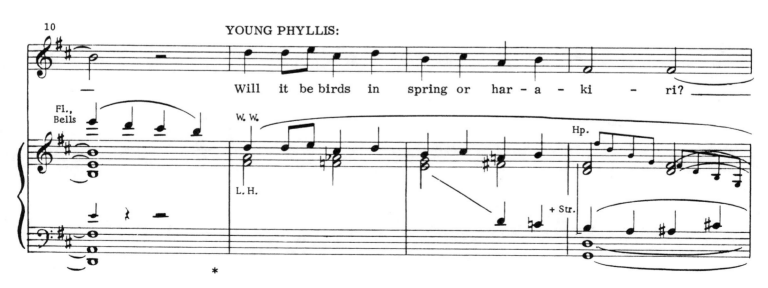

now will be the best day you ev - er had. _____

*(Y.P. opt. 8va)

YOUNG BEN:
You're gon-na love to - mor-row. __ You're gon-na be with me. _

YOUNG PHYLLIS:
(W.W.)
Mm - hm. Mm -

208

No.19-2a

Tomorrow-Exit

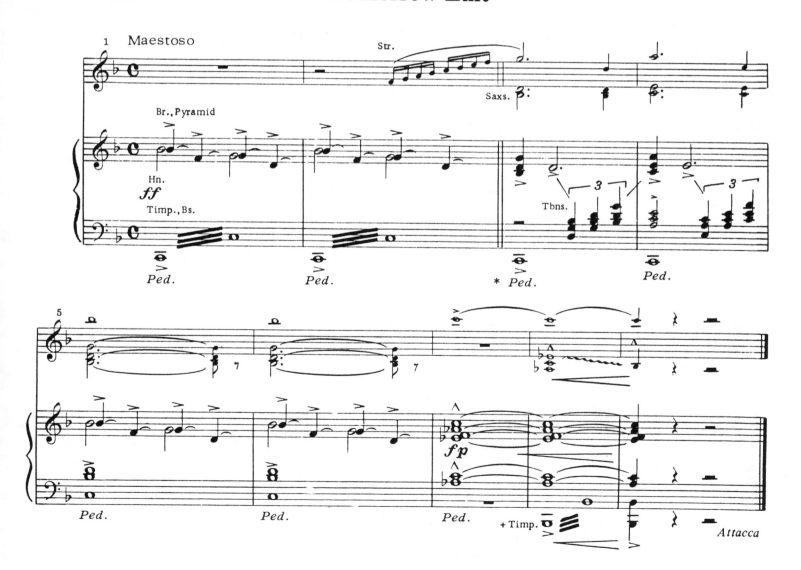

Buddy's Blues

(Buddy, 2 Girls)

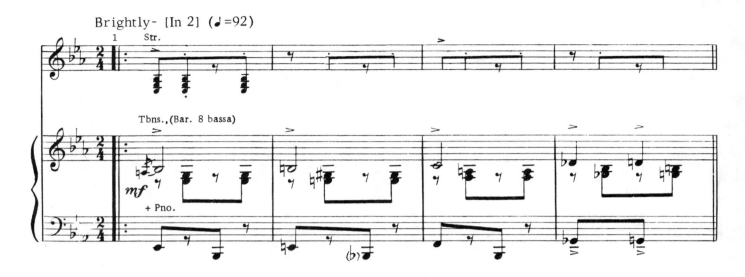

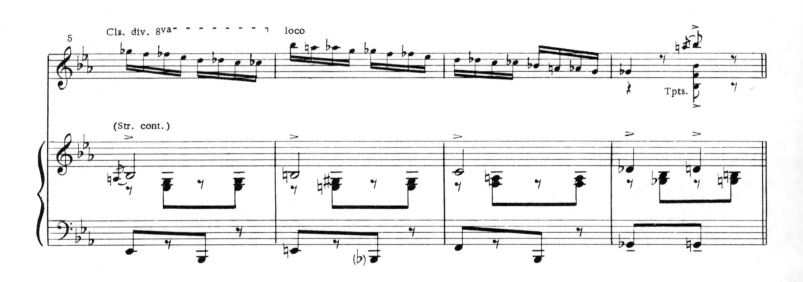

212

nore me, you're the on - ly thing that mat -ters" Feel - ing. ____

That "If I'm good e - nough for you, you're

not good e - nough" ___ And "Thank you for the pres - ent, but what's

wrong with it?" stuff. ___ Those "Don't come an - y clos - er 'cause you

216

ings, _____ Those "Go a - way, I need you,"

"Come to me, I'll kill you," "Dar - ling, I'll do an - y - thing to keep you with me

till you tell me that you love me, oh you did, now beat it,

will you?" Blues. _____

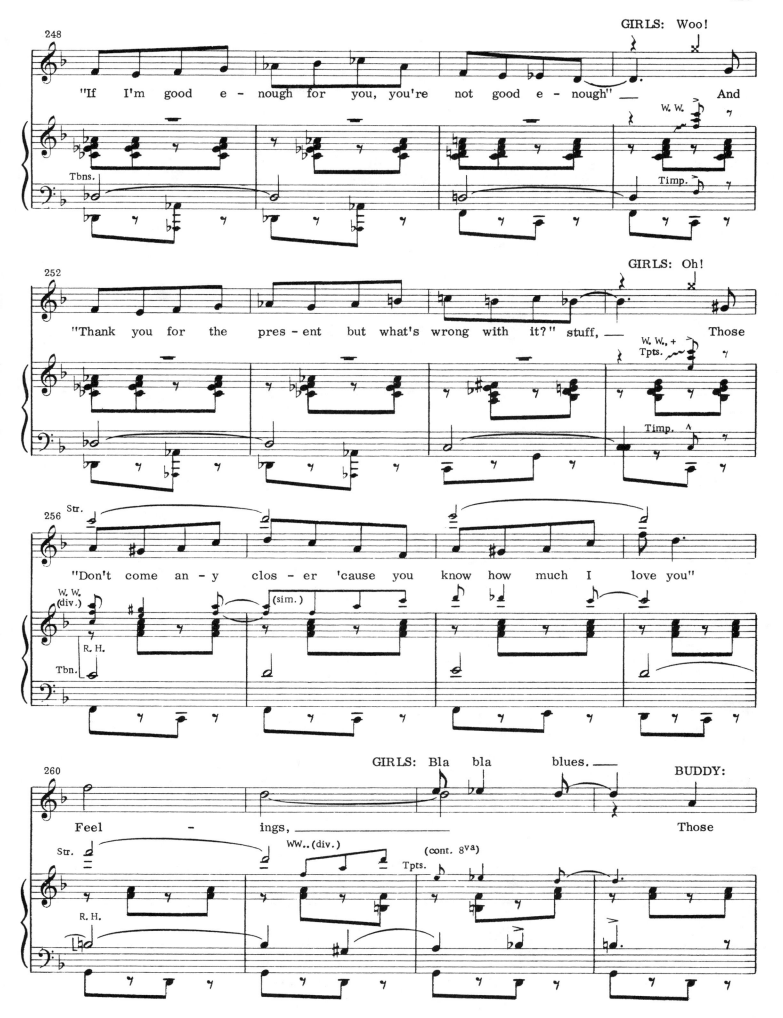

GIRLS: Woo!

"If I'm good e-nough for you, you're not good e-nough" ___ And

GIRLS: Oh!

"Thank you for the pres-ent but what's wrong with it?" stuff, ___ Those

"Don't come an-y clos-er 'cause you know how much I love you"

GIRLS: Bla bla blues. ___ BUDDY:

Feel - ings, _____ Those

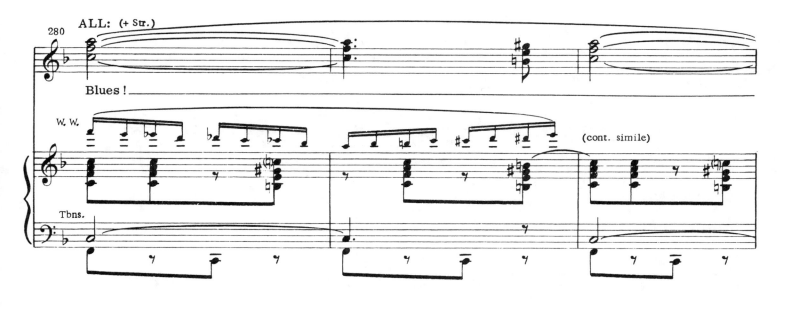

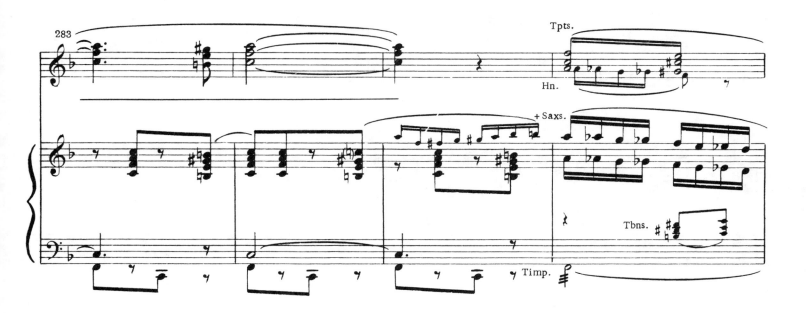

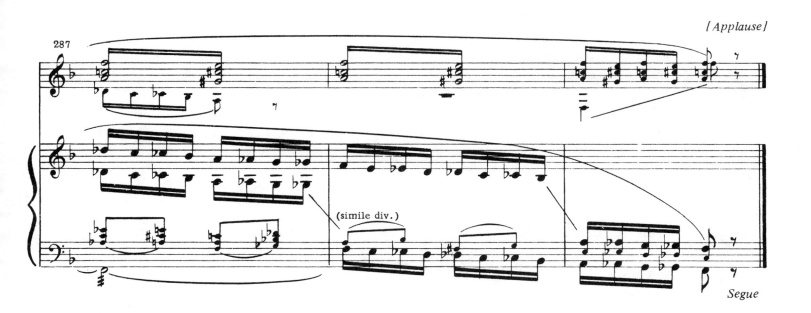

No. 19-4

Losing My Mind
(Sally)

Cue: After applause from "Buddy's Blues"

The sun comes up, I think about you. The coffee cup, I think about

you. I want you so, It's like I'm losing my mind.

The morning ends, I think about you. I talk to friends, I think about

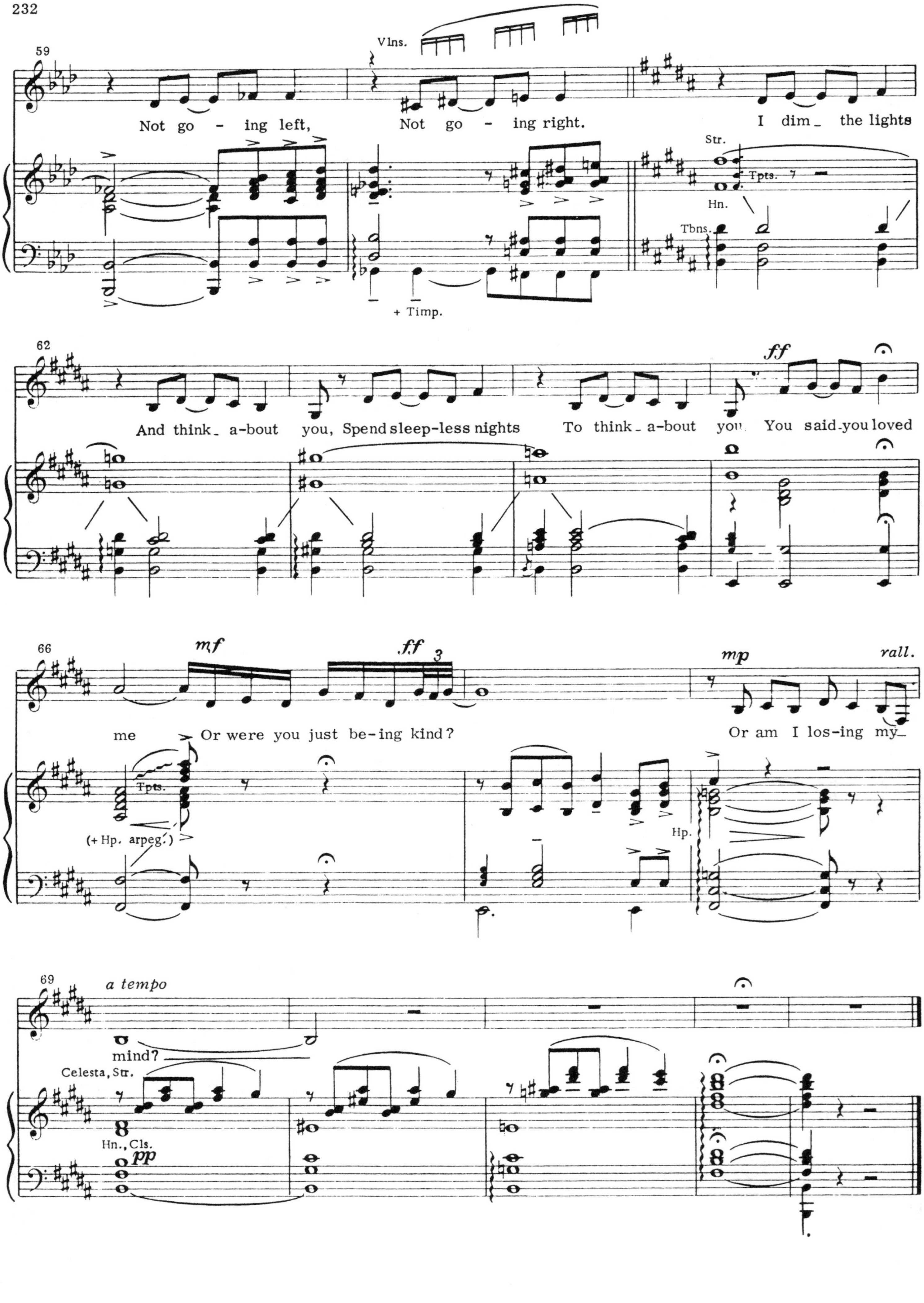
59
Vlns.
Not go - ing left,
Not go - ing right.
I dim_ the lights
Str.
Tpts.
Hn.
Tbns.
+ Timp.
62
ff
And think_ a-bout you, Spend sleep-less nights
To think_ a-bout you. You said_you loved
66
mf
ff
3
mp
rall.
me
Or were you just be-ing kind?
Or am I los-ing my_
Tpts.
(+ Hp. arpeg.)
Hp.
69
a tempo
mind?
Celesta, Str.
Hn., Cls.
pp

No. 19-5

Lucy And Jessie
(Phyllis)

Here's a lit - tle sto - ry that should make you cry,__ A-bout

two un - hap - py dames.__ Let us call them Luc - y "X" and

Jes - sie "Y,"__ which are not their re - al names.__ Now

Jes - sie wants to be juic - y. Luc - y wants to be Jes - sie and Jes - sie, Luc - y. You see,

Jes - sie is rac - y, but hard as a rock. Luc - y is lac - y, but

dull as a smock. Jes - sie wants to be lac - y, Luc - y wants to be Jes - sie.

That's the sor - row - ful pré - cis. It's ver - y mess - y.

240

Tell 'em that they ought to get to - geth-er quick,_ 'Cause get - ting it to-geth - er is the

whole _____ trick, yeah!

242

No. 19-6

Live, Laugh, Love

(Ben, Chorus)

Of all the things they've ris - en a - bove. _____

Some like to be pro - found _ By read - ing Proust and Pound. _

Me, I like to live, Me, I like to laugh, Me, I like to love. _____

Suc - cess is swell _ And suc - cess is _ sweet, _ But

Don't give up the ship. _____ No. Learn how to laugh, Learn how_

_ to love, Learn how to live, That's my tip._

When I hear the rum -bling, _ Yes? Do I lose my grip? _____ No.

I have to laugh, I have _ to love, I have to live. That's my trip._

When the wind is blow-ing, _____ That's the time to smile. _____

When the rent is ow - ing, _____ Nev - er lose your style. _____

Some get a boot from shoot-ing off ca-ble-grams __

Or buzz-ing bells to sum-mon the staff. _____

Some climb-ers get their kicks __ From so-cial pol-i-tics. __

[Conductor tries to cue Ben on the lyrics]

Me, I like to live, Me, I like to love, Me, I ___

151

cess is swell ___ And suc - cess is ___ sweet. ___ But

+ Str., W. W.

+ Tbns.

155

ev - 'ry height ___ has a drop. _____ The

159

[Stop at cue: BEN: I only wanted her until I had her. *] Segue to* 19-7

less a - chieve - ment, The less de - feat. ___

162

[Safety bars]

What's the point of shov-in' your way to the top? ___

W. W.

Tpts., Str.

Cue: BEN: After that - -

Finale-Chaos

No. 19-7a

Finale-Addenda
(Chaos)

[Stage Band]

Cue: CARLOTTA: What this party needs is a kick in the ass.

[2 starts]

First time - stop as Ben comes through the dancers and
                    goes to their left.
Second time - start at cue: BEN: Phyllis.
Second time - stop when chant begins "Juicy Lucy, Dressy Jessie" etc.

No. 19-8

Curtain

Cue: PHYLLIS: Bet your ass.

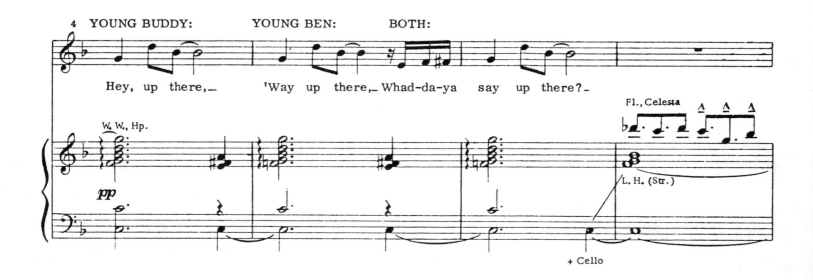

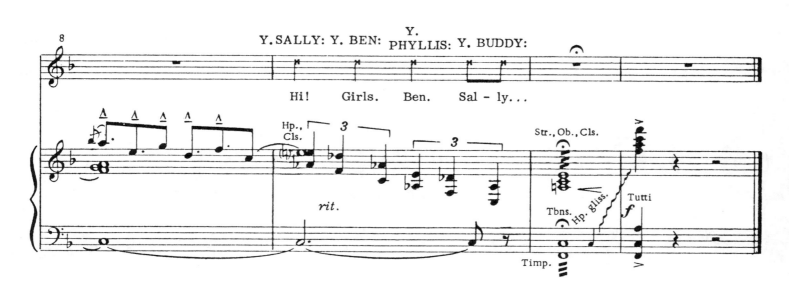

No. 20

Bows

(Including "Exit Music")

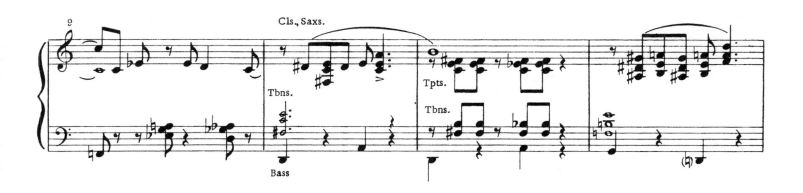